The Struggle for EQUALITY

1955–1975

Ann M. Rossi

PICTURE CREDITS
Cover (background), page 4–5 Robert W. Kelley/Time Life Pictures/Getty Images; cover (inset) Photri-Microstock; pages 2–3, 3 (border), 7 (border), 12, 13 (border), 14 (bottom), 17 (border) 25 (border), 33 (border), 38, 39 (border), 40 (border) Flip Schulke/Corbis; pages 2–3 John Olson/Time Life Pictures/Getty Images; pages 4, 17, 19 (top), 21, 26, 30 (right), 34 (bottom), 36 (bottom) AP Wide World Photos; page 6 Carl Iwasaki/Time Life Pictures/Getty Images; page 7 Eve Arnold/Magnum Photos; page 8 George Silk/Time Life Pictures/Getty Images; pags 9 (top and bottom), 10, 13, 15, 28 (top and bottom), 29, 34 (top) Bettmann/Corbis; page 14 (top) Courtesy of the Library of Congress; pages 16, 25 Corbis; pages 18, 19 (bottom) Arthur Schatz/Time Life Pictures/Getty Images; pages 20–21 Farrell Greehan/Corbis; page 22 David Butow/Corbis SABA; page 23 Tony Arruza/Corbis; page 24 Duomo/Corbis; page 27 Ralph Crane/Time Life Pictures/Getty Images; page 30 (left) Wolfgang Kaehler/Corbis; page 31 Ed Kashi/Corbis; page 32 Mike Zens/Corbis; page 33 Shelley Gazin/Corbis; page 35 TK; page 36 (top) Bill Pierce/Time Life Pictures/Getty Images; page 37 Jeffrey Markowitz/Corbis Sygma.

QUOTATIONS
page 11 Martin Luther King, Jr. from, "Letter from Birmingham Jail," April 16, 1963; page 12 Fannie Lou Hamer from *Voices of Freedom: An Oral History of the Civil Rights Movement from the 1950s through the 1980s* by Henry Hampton and Steve Fayer with Sarah Flynn; page 18 Cesar Chavez from http://clnet.ucr.edu/research/chavez/bio; page 19 Dolores Huerta from http://www.ufw.org/dh.htm; page 21 José Angel Gutiérrez; page 35 Mariah Burton Nelson from *The Stronger Women Get, the More Men Love Football: Sexism and the American Culture of Sports* by Mariah Burton Nelson.

Produced through the worldwide resources of the National Geographic Society, John M. Fahey, Jr., President and Chief Executive Officer; Gilbert M. Grosvenor, Chairman of the Board; Nina D. Hoffman, Executive Vice President and President, Books and Education Publishing Group.

PREPARED BY NATIONAL GEOGRAPHIC SCHOOL PUBLISHING
Ericka Markman, Senior Vice President and President, Children's Books and Education Publishing Group; Steve Mico, Vice President, Editorial Director; Marianne Hiland, Executive Editor; Anita Schwartz, Project Editor, Jim Hiscott, Design Manager; Kristin Hanneman, Illustrations Manager; Diana Bourdrez, Picture Editor; Matt Wascavage, Manager of Publishing Services; Sean Philpotts, Production Manager.

MANUFACTURING AND QUALITY MANAGEMENT
Christopher A. Liedel, Chief Financial Officer;
Phillip L. Schlosser, Director; Clifton M. Brown III, Manager.

PROGRAM DEVELOPMENT Gare Thompson Associates, Inc.

CONSULTANTS/REVIEWERS
Dr. Margit E. McGuire, School of Education, Seattle University, Seattle, Washington; Dr. Russell Adams, Dept. of Afro-American Studies, Howard University, Washington, D.C.

BOOK DEVELOPMENT Nieman Inc.

BOOK DESIGN Three Communication Design, LLC

ART DIRECTOR Dan Banks, Project Design Company

MAP DEVELOPMENT AND PRODUCTION Bruce Burdick

Published by the National Geographic Society
Washington, D.C. 20036-4688

Product No. 4J41753

ISBN-13: 978-0-7922-4559-9
ISBN-10: 0-7922-4559-8

Printed in the United States of America

24 23 22 21 20 19 18
15 14 13 12 11 10 9

Table of Contents

"The heart of the question is whether all Americans are to [receive] equal rights and equal opportunities, whether we are going to treat our fellow Americans as we want to be treated."

—PRESIDENT JOHN F. KENNEDY

The chief of police of McComb, Mississippi, enforces segregation at a bus station in 1961.

Introduction

The Fourteenth Amendment to the U.S. Constitution was passed in 1868. It guaranteed citizenship rights to all people born in the United States. However, this amendment did not end **discrimination**, or unfair treatment. Many people continued to show prejudice toward **minority** groups and women. Various states had passed laws that required different treatment of certain groups of people.

Minority groups and women have had to fight for their **civil rights**. Civil rights, such as freedom from discrimination, are guaranteed to citizens by the Constitution and by acts of Congress. They include equal treatment under the law and voting rights. By the 1950s, African Americans felt that they had been denied these rights far too long. They started the civil rights movement.

During the 1950s and early 1960s, African Americans used both the law and non-violent protest to gain their civil rights. In the later 1960s, some leaders, impatient with the progress of the movement, wanted to use violence.

At the same time, other groups were fighting for their rights too. Latinos, Native Americans, and women pursued their own struggles for equality. All these struggles changed America.

More than 200,000 people joined in the civil rights March on Washington in August 1963.

The African-American Challenge

Chapter 1

In 1896, the Supreme Court, the highest court in the land, ruled that states could have "separate but equal" facilities for blacks and whites. This meant that racial **segregation** was legal. By the early 1900s, laws in every southern state required segregation, or the separation of blacks and whites in public places. The problem was that places for blacks in parks, trains, schools, and other public places were almost never as good as places for whites.

People who thought segregation was wrong founded the National Association for the Advancement of Colored People (NAACP) in 1909. Lawyers for the NAACP fought many legal battles to end discrimination. One very important case was *Brown v. Board of Education of Topeka.*

Linda Brown was an African-American girl living in Topeka, Kansas. Only whites could go to the public school near her home. So, Linda had to take a bus to an all-black school. The Browns and other African-American families decided to sue the school district.

Thurgood Marshall (center), with other NAACP lawyers, fought for school desegregation.

Thurgood Marshall was a lawyer for the NAACP. He argued that the Fourteenth Amendment said that states must treat all citizens alike. He said that black children did not get the same schooling as white children. "Separate" could never be "equal." On May 17, 1954, the Supreme Court ruled that school segregation was **unconstitutional**. This meant that separating citizens on the basis of race was illegal in *all* public places and institutions. As a result, great changes were about to take place.

◀ Linda Brown sits in her segregated classroom.

Trouble in Little Rock

Despite the 1954 Supreme Court ruling, most schools did not end segregation quickly. In 1957, Arkansas governor Orval Faubus refused to end segregation in Little Rock Central High School. When school opened on September 3, Governor Faubus ordered Arkansas National Guardsmen to keep African-American students out of the school.

Faubus claimed he was protecting the nine black students who wanted to enroll. However, some people pointed out that Faubus hoped to be re-elected. He needed the support of white voters. Most of them wanted segregated schools.

On September 4, one of the nine students, 15-year-old Elizabeth Eckford, arrived at Central High School. Elizabeth had to walk through a huge crowd of screaming white people. Armed guards turned her away from the school.

Finally, on September 23, Faubus ordered police to escort the students into the school. The mob was too angry for the police to control. President Dwight D. Eisenhower then ordered army troops to take the African-American students to school and protect them. The federal government had shown that it would defend civil rights.

President Eisenhower ordered troops to escort the Little Rock Nine safely to school.

Boycotts and Sit-ins

Often, African Americans held protests to draw attention to their unfair treatment. A protest is a public display of disapproval for an idea or action.

In Montgomery, Alabama, in 1955, buses were segregated. Black people had to ride in the back of a bus. They had to give up their seats to whites if a bus was crowded. In December 1955, an African-American woman named Rosa Parks refused to give a white man her seat on the bus. She was arrested. The angry black community organized a bus boycott. For over a year, more than 40,000 people in Montgomery didn't ride the buses. The bus companies lost a lot of money.

A policeman drags a sit-in demonstrator out of a restaurant in Cambridge, Maryland, in 1963.

In November 1956, the Supreme Court ruled that bus segregation in Alabama was unconstitutional. After that, black passengers could sit anywhere they wished.

Sit-ins were another kind of peaceful protest. In 1960, four African-American college students in North Carolina went into a lunch counter and ordered food. The waitress would not serve them.

As the days passed, more students sat at the lunch counter. Soon, students were holding sit-ins all over the South. Then, people all over the country refused to shop in stores that would not serve both blacks and whites. Before long, stores began to change their policies.

Meet | Martin Luther King, Jr.

The African Americans in Montgomery chose Martin Luther King, Jr., as the leader of the bus boycott. A minister, King urged African Americans to boycott the buses peacefully. King's call for non-violent action helped make him famous.

Tensions in Birmingham

Not all protests were peaceful. In April 1963, civil rights leaders decided to protest segregation in Birmingham, Alabama. Segregationists had bombed African-American parts of town so often that some people called the city "Bombingham."

Martin Luther King, Jr., and other leaders planned a peaceful march for May 2. Around a thousand children marched. Some were only six years old. Police arrested most of them.

Protesters marched again the next day. This time, police dogs attacked them. Firefighters sprayed them with water from high-powered hoses. Television newscasts brought these horrors into American homes. Newspapers showed photos of people being knocked down by jets of water from hoses and bitten by dogs.

The protests went on for days. Some people threw rocks at police. Thousands of marchers, including 600 children, were jailed. On May 10, city leaders agreed to desegregate.

The agreement angered many whites. Bombs destroyed civil rights offices and the home of King's brother. In response, more than 100,000 people took part in demonstrations over the next several months.

Children are arrested for protesting in Birmingham.

Kennedy speaks in Houston.

The Civil Rights Act of 1964

About a month after the protests in Birmingham, President John F. Kennedy spoke to the nation. He wanted Congress to pass a bill to end racial discrimination. Civil rights leaders wanted to show their support for the bill. They planned a march on Washington, D.C.

About 250,000 people joined the march on August 28, 1963. Many were white. The crowd listened to many speakers. Finally, they heard Martin Luther King, Jr., give his famous "I Have a Dream" speech.

Just a few months later, in November 1963, President Kennedy was **assassinated**, or murdered. His Vice President, Lyndon Johnson, became President. He convinced Congress to pass the Civil Rights Act of 1964. This bill banned segregation in public places. It also banned employment discrimination based on a person's race, color, religion, sex, or national origin.

Voices from America

"Injustice anywhere is a threat to justice everywhere."

—MARTIN LUTHER KING, JR., 1963

The Right to Vote

The Civil Rights Act of 1964 banned discrimination. In many parts of the South, African Americans still could not vote. In Mississippi, for example, whites stopped African Americans from registering to vote. They asked people who could not read or write to fill out questionnaires. African Americans who registered often lost their jobs.

During the "Freedom Summer" of 1964, hundreds of blacks and whites came from all over the country to Mississippi. They helped African Americans register to vote.

Black voters line up outside a polling place in Alabama in 1966.

The Freedom Summer of 1964 had an important result. President Johnson persuaded Congress to pass the Voting Rights Act of 1965. This tough new law said states could not use reading and writing tests or other means to keep people from voting. It ensured African Americans' right to vote.

Things got better quickly. Within months, there were about 250,000 new African-American voters. That year in Mississippi, more African-American leaders were elected than in any other state. Within five years, the total number of voters in the South had nearly doubled.

Voices from America

"I traveled 26 miles to the county courthouse to try to register. I was fired from a plantation where I had worked as a timekeeper and a sharecropper for 18 years."

—FANNIE LOU HAMER, 1964

The Civil Rights Movement Expands

Chapter 2

In the 1960s, the civil rights movement spread from the South to cities across the United States. Many African Americans lived in crowded city slums. Black newcomers were directed to low-rent sections of a city. They did not choose to live there, but often, the only place blacks could rent or buy were in the run-down parts of a city.

In 1965, African Americans rioted in Watts, a section of Los Angeles, California. They were tired of being treated unfairly. Martin Luther King, Jr., asked the people of Watts to protest peacefully. They booed him.

Then, riots took place in Chicago during the hot summer of 1966. Shortly after the riots, Martin Luther King, Jr., and other civil rights leaders led a series of marches into Chicago's white neighborhoods. They wanted to draw attention to segregated housing. Angry white mobs threw rocks, bricks, and bottles at the marchers. The marches continued for more than a month. Finally, Chicago's mayor, Richard J. Daley, agreed to work on the housing problem. Years later, however, housing conditions in black communities remained essentially unchanged.

National Guardsmen patrol the streets following riots in Chicago.

Malcolm X and Black Power

As the 1960s continued, so did black community demonstrations in Newark, Detroit, Cleveland, and other northern cities. Many African Americans were angry. Civil rights laws had been passed. Yet, the lives of many black people had not changed. Most were still poor. Most still lived in poor housing.

Some African Americans believed that non-violent protests were not working. An African-American leader, Malcolm X, was one of them. He did not believe in non-violent protest. "Non-violence is the philosophy of a fool," he said. A powerful speaker, Malcolm X became a symbol of what was later called the Black Power Movement. In time, however, he was willing to work with other civil rights leaders on some issues. He died before he saw many improvements in African-American lives, however. He was only 39 in 1965 when he was assassinated.

Malcolm X speaks to reporters.

Meet | **Stokely Carmichael**

At first, Stokely Carmichael was in favor of a non-violent approach to gaining civil rights. He was arrested more than 30 times for taking part in marches and demonstrations in the South. Over time, he became angry at the slow progress blacks seemed to be making. In 1966, he was the first to call for "Black Power" during a speech in Mississippi.

Marchers at the funeral of Dr. Martin Luther King, Jr.

The Death of Martin Luther King

Many African Americans liked the term "Black Power." It made them feel proud to be black. Others disliked the term because they thought it sounded violent. Black Power divided the civil rights movement.

Martin Luther King, Jr., did not like the term "Black Power." It frightened many white supporters of the civil rights movement. He continued to urge people to use non-violence to protest. In April 1968, he became a victim of violence himself.

King went to Memphis, Tennessee. He wanted to show his support for African-American sanitation workers. They had stopped work to get better working conditions. King was murdered on April 4 while standing on the balcony of his motel room. All over the country, people mourned his senseless murder. In anger and frustration, African Americans rioted in more than 100 cities.

A few months later, the Civil Rights Act of 1968 became law. This law was also known as the Fair Housing Act. It said that no one could be stopped from buying or renting housing because of his or her race.

Barbara Jordan, the first African-American female senator in Texas, was elected to the U.S. House of Representatives in 1972.

Effect of the Struggle

Those who fought for civil rights were heroes. Some of them lost their lives in the struggle. Through their brave efforts, African Americans won important rights. Schools were forced to desegregate. Laws banned segregation and discrimination in housing. The federal government helped to enforce these laws. As a result, many African Americans could get a good education, better jobs, and improved housing.

The Voting Rights Act of 1965 helped African Americans win power in their communities. They were able to elect many African Americans to office. In 1966, Barbara Jordan became the first black state senator in Texas since 1883. Maynard H. Jackson became the first black mayor of Atlanta in 1973. That same year, Thomas Bradley became the first black mayor of Los Angeles. Black leaders continue to play important roles in Congress and in many cities today.

Latinos Struggle for Rights

Chapter 3

African Americans were not the only group to be discriminated against in the United States. Latinos are people of Spanish-speaking heritage. They also faced segregation and poverty in the 1950s and 1960s. Most worked at low-paying jobs or could not find work at all. Many lived in poor housing.

A great many Latinos lived in the Southwest and were Mexican Americans. Some Mexican-American families had lived in the United States for generations. However, they were not allowed to eat in restaurants or drink from water fountains that whites used. Public restrooms and swimming pools were for whites only. Mexican-American children were not allowed to speak Spanish in school. Often, they were punished if they did.

Like African Americans, many Mexican Americans had served in World War II. As war veterans who had fought for their country, they wanted to be treated fairly. They wanted to end discrimination. Many Mexican Americans joined together to fight poverty and discrimination.

Some Latino workers lived in company-owned camps.

César Chávez

Mexican Americans had long worked on farms in the West and Southwest. Farm work was hard and dirty. It paid very little. Workers tried to win better working conditions by banding together. They had little success until César Chávez (CHAH-vez) became their leader. He worked hard to gain basic rights for farm workers.

César Chávez (center front) stands with a group of farm workers

César Chávez was born in Arizona in 1927. His parents had a small farm but lost it in the Depression, a period of hard times and high unemployment in the 1930s. When Chávez was ten, his parents became **migrants**. They traveled from place to place to work at planting and harvesting. Chávez left school after the eighth grade to work in the fields. He learned firsthand the brutal conditions of migrant farm workers' lives. These workers often lived in shacks with no running water, electricity, or bathrooms. Their work was dangerous, and they had no protection.

After serving in World War II, Chávez married and settled in California. Once again, he worked in the fields. Then, he began to work with a Latino civil rights group. Chávez met someone there who shared his views: Dolores Huerta (HWAIR-tuh).

Voices from America

"I couldn't stand seeing kids come to class hungry and needing shoes. I thought I could do more by organizing farm workers than by trying to teach their hungry children."

—DOLORES HUERTA

Dolores Huerta worked to improve the lives of farm workers.

Dolores Huerta

Dolores Huerta was born in New Mexico in 1930, but grew up in Stockton, California. After her parents divorced, her mother raised the family. Huerta's mother owned a restaurant and hotel. She often let farm workers stay there for free. From her mother, Huerta learned to be kind and caring. She also learned to be an outspoken activist. She worked hard to stop injustice.

After college, Huerta was a teacher in a farm workers' community. Huerta saw how hungry the children were. Their families were poor. Huerta wanted to do something to help them. Soon, she was fighting to end segregation. She led efforts to get Latinos to vote, and she worked for better public services. She also became a lobbyist, persuading lawmakers to pass laws that helped farm workers. One of the laws gave voters the right to vote in Spanish. Another law helped injured farm workers get insurance.

Dolores Huerta

The Farm Workers Movement

In 1962, Dolores Huerta and César Chávez co-founded the National Farm Workers Association (NFWA). This organization later became the United Farm Workers (UFW). Chávez and Huerta believed that farm workers needed to unionize, or join together. Then, they could win better living and working conditions.

Like Martin Luther King, Jr., Huerta and Chávez believed in non-violent ways of making changes. In 1965, Chávez led NFWA members in a strike. They were supporting striking Filipino grape pickers. The next year, Chávez asked shoppers across the country to boycott grapes. Many people stopped buying grapes.

By 1970, the grape pickers' strike had become the longest in American history. At last, most grape growers agreed to give workers better pay and better working conditions.

After this success, Chávez and Huerta did the same thing for workers who picked lettuce. They asked people not to buy lettuce. Finally, in 1975, California passed a law giving farm workers greater rights to deal with employers. Now, workers had a chance for a better life.

Grape workers on strike picketing in Delano, California

La Raza Unida

During the 1960s and 1970s, Mexican Americans living in the Southwest needed more political influence. Many worked to gain this influence. In 1961, Henry B. Gonzalez, a Latino from Texas, was elected to the U.S. Congress. Joseph Montoya was elected to the U.S. Senate from New Mexico in 1964.

Latino leaders formed many different groups. One group was La Raza Unida (The United People). José Angel Gutiérrez and others started this group in Texas in 1970.

Voices from America

"We no longer accept the fact that we are powerless . . . We know we're powerful, we know we can be organized, we know we can triumph."

—JOSÉ ANGEL GUTIÉRREZ

In 1971, La Raza Unida candidates won local elections in several Texas cities. La Raza Unida became a national political party. Gutiérrez became its leader in 1972. That same year, La Raza Unida ran candidates for several state offices in Texas.

Although La Raza Unida no longer exists, it was important. It inspired some Latinos to run for political office. Others were encouraged to register to vote. Large numbers of Mexican Americans have been supporters of the nation's two main political parties.

Students learn in a bilingual classroom with Spanish and English on the posters.

Bilingual Education

Latinos in the United States knew that school was important. Only education could make their lives better. One program for Latino students was **bilingual** education. The federal government first funded bilingual education programs in 1968.

Bilingual education for Spanish-speaking students means they are taught basic subjects, such as math and science, in Spanish. At the same time, these students study English as a second language. Then, when the students improve their English, they join classes that are taught only in English. The goal of bilingual education is to keep students from falling behind in important subjects while they learn English.

Some people did not support bilingual education. They thought that bilingual programs discouraged Latino students from learning English. People in favor of bilingual education said that the government was not giving enough money for it. Even today, many people do not agree about the value of bilingual education.

The Latino Population Grows

Especially during the 1950s, Latinos came to the United States from Puerto Rico, Cuba, and Central America. Some came to find work. Others came to find safety from revolutions and wars. All wanted a better life for themselves and their families.

Hundreds of thousands of people from Puerto Rico came to the United States to find jobs. Most of them settled in New York City.

In 1959, Fidel Castro became the dictator of Cuba. Many Cubans then fled their country. Most of them settled in Florida. Some were wealthy and well educated.

In the 1970s, people from Central America began to come to the United States. These new arrivals faced problems. Most were not educated, and they spoke little or no English. They had a hard time finding work and housing. Yet, thousands of immigrants continue to arrive.

Children play at a multicultural street festival in Coconut Grove, Florida.

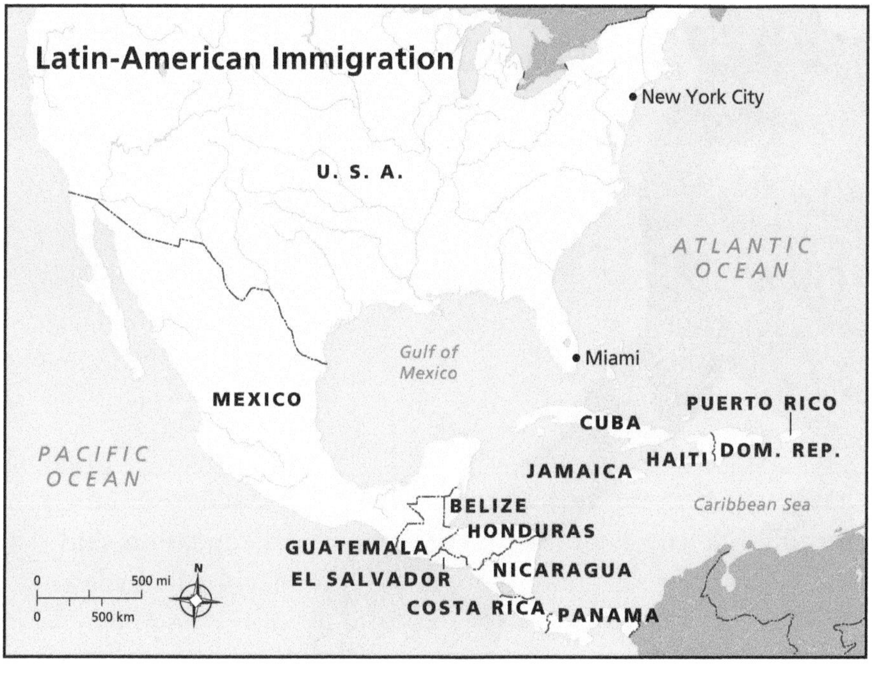

Results of the Latino Struggle

Latino leaders worked hard to improve the lives of their people. They won the support of many non-Latinos. Boycotts led by César Chávez and Dolores Huerta led to better working conditions and better pay for farm workers.

Voter registration drives encouraged more Latinos to vote. The Voting Rights Act of 1965 also helped Latinos elect political candidates. During the 1960s, four Mexican Americans were elected to Congress. These four people were strong supporters of civil rights. Today, hundreds of Latinos hold political offices in the United States. Thousands more have successful businesses. Still other Latinos have become famous athletes, entertainers, and writers.

Latinos still face some problems. Discrimination against Latinos has not ended. New arrivals often do not have the job skills they need. Latino students who do not speak English have a hard time in school. Many Latinos live in poverty. Today, Latinos continue the struggle to improve their lives.

Latino Alex Rodriguez is one of the highest-paid players in major league baseball.

Native Americans Demand Justice

Chapter 4

Before white settlers arrived in North America, Native Americans lived according to their own traditions. For example, they believed that a community of people shared the land around them. White settlers, however, did not want to share land. They wanted to own it. They wanted land for farms, ranches, and mines. Over time, they took it away from Native Americans.

Native American children pose for a photo at the Carlisle Indian School in Pennsylvania.

During the 1700s and 1800s, the United States government signed many treaties, or agreements, with Native American tribes. Over and over again, such treaties were broken. Native-Americans were forced off their lands to make room for white settlers.

The government also passed several laws to force Native Americans onto reservations. Native American children were sent to boarding schools run by the government. These schools tried to turn Indian children into "American" children. Many children were well educated. At the same time, their Indian culture was ignored. This made Native Americans angry. They did not want to give up their traditions or their languages. They wanted to win back land and their rights as citizens.

INDIANS
WELCOME
UNITED INDIAN
PROPERTY
ALCATRAZ ISLAND AREA 12 ACRES
1½ MILES TO TRANSPORT DOCK
ALLOWED ASHORE
WITHOUT A PASS
INDIAN LAND

Pushing for Rights

During the 1960s and 1970s, several Native American groups worked to win their rights. One of these groups was the American Indian Movement (AIM). AIM fought for more and better jobs for Native Americans. It worked to make schools and medical services better. AIM encouraged Indians to keep their traditional culture alive. It asked for the return of lands that had been taken from them.

During the 1960s and 1970s, AIM and other groups led some important protests. Sometimes, they worked within the law. At other times, they worked outside the law. The groups wanted to make sure the government responded to their demands. Native Americans won an important right in 1968. The Civil Rights Act of 1968 granted all Native Americans full civil rights.

Native Americans dance during the occupation of Alcatraz Island in 1969.

The Seizure of Alcatraz

AIM was involved in a protest that took place on Alcatraz Island in San Francisco Bay. The federal government owned Alcatraz Island. It had been used as a federal prison for many years but was closed in 1963. In March 1964, members of the Sioux (Soo) nation claimed the island. They said they had an 1868 treaty with the federal government. They believed this treaty gave them Alcatraz along with other land.

In November 1969, 78 Native Americans landed on the island. This group represented several tribes. They wanted to make people aware of the problems Indians faced. Poverty and poor housing on the reservations were some of the problems. The group succeeded in getting publicity, but in June 1971, federal marshals removed them from the island.

Native Americans stake their claim to land on Alcatraz Island in San Francisco Bay.

The Standoff at Wounded Knee

On February 27, 1973, members of AIM led another takeover. With several hundred Sioux Indians, they occupied the village of Wounded Knee, South Dakota. The village was on a reservation of the Oglala Sioux. The federal government ran the reservation. Wounded Knee had a terrible history. In 1890, the United States cavalry killed more than 200 Sioux men, women, and children at Wounded Knee.

In 1973, Native Americans renamed the village the "Independent Oglala Sioux Nation." They made many demands. They were angry about all the years of abuse they had suffered. They told the government that it would either have to discuss their demands or remove the protesters by force.

Federal agents soon surrounded Wounded Knee. Two Native Americans were killed, and one U.S. marshal was seriously injured. Newspapers and magazines covered the events. Soon, people around the world knew about the Native Americans' fight for their rights. On May 8, after 71 days, those occupying Wounded Knee left. The U.S. government had finally agreed to discuss their demands.

AIM leaders meet with government negotiators to end the standoff at Wounded Knee.

Meet | **Russell Means**

Born on the Pine Ridge Reservation in South Dakota, Russell Means is an Oglala Sioux. Means became famous because he was the leader of the standoff at Wounded Knee. He was arrested as a result, but a judge dismissed the charges. Means later became an actor. He continues to be an activist, speaking on Indian affairs at colleges.

Winning Back Indian Land

An Indian chief and his translator witness President Richard Nixon's signing of a bill giving the Taos Indians title to their land.

In 1946, Congress passed a law setting up the Indian Claims Commission. This was a court that Native American tribes could go to if they believed that the government had wrongly taken their land. The Commission could not return land to a tribe. Instead, it could pay for the land if it decided that land had been taken wrongly.

Sometimes, the tribes did not want money. They wanted their land back. The Taos Pueblo Indians of New Mexico fought for the return of the Blue Lake area of New Mexico. The U.S. government had taken this 48,000-acre area in 1906 to become part of a national forest. The Taos people consider Blue Lake a sacred place. They refused any money from the government. In 1970, they were successful in getting the land back.

Native Americans won their largest land settlement in Alaska. The United States had bought Alaska from Russia in 1867. Nothing was done about the land claims of the native peoples of Alaska for many years. In 1966, Native Americans in Alaska asked to have their claims settled. In 1971, they were successful. They won 44 million acres of land and almost one billion dollars.

Nez Perce Indians returning to former tribal lands in Oregon

More court cases in several areas of the United States followed. They were not all successful, but many were. They were an important step in the Native American fight for rights.

Ruins of the Puye Cliff Dwellings in a Native American land settlement in New Mexico

Native Americans and Education

In the 1960s, Native American leaders focused on urging their people to stay in school. They encouraged students to get college degrees. They also wanted Indian education to benefit Indians.

In 1975, Congress passed a law that allowed Indian tribes to run their own programs. These programs were for education, child welfare, family services, and health. They were also for housing and law enforcement. The government paid for the programs.

Education was an important part of this law. In earlier years, the U.S. government had decided what to teach Indian children. Now, Native Americans could decide how to educate their own people. This law gave them money for that purpose.

Native American school in Washington

Native Americans preserving their traditions at an inter-tribal powwow in Cashmere, Washington

Victories and the Continuing Struggle

Native Americans have made progress in getting their rights. They have regained some of their lands. Tribal governments on reservations have the right to govern their lands and control their own businesses. Native American children today are learning more about their own traditions.

Yet, Native Americans continue to face many problems. Poverty and unemployment are widespread. Native Americans worry that their languages and culture are vanishing. To end discrimination, some groups try to teach other Americans about their culture. They hope knowledge will lead to respect.

Tribes have rented the use of their land to government and to private companies. They have put money from land-claim settlements into building businesses. Also, federal funding has helped some Native Americans to start their own companies.

Women Battle for Equality

Chapter 5

During the 1960s and 1970s, women also fought for equal rights. Betty Friedan (free-DAN) was a leader in that battle. Before Friedan went to her 15th college reunion, she sent questionnaires to 200 members of her class. She asked the women to describe their lives after college.

Their answers surprised Friedan. Most of the women had become housewives. Many felt that something was missing from their lives. Friedan did research. Then, she wrote a book called *The Feminine Mystique.*

Published in 1963, the book quickly became a best-seller. In her book, Friedan wrote that society had forced most women to be wives and mothers. Most ads and magazines showed women only as happy mothers and wives. Friedan said many middle-class women were not satisfied with those roles. What they really wanted and needed was work outside the home. Friedan also said that women with careers were not treated with respect. They were paid less than men. Many jobs were not open to women, especially not to minority women.

Betty Friedan

The National Organization for Women

After *The Feminine Mystique* was published, Friedan received hundreds of letters from women. Many agreed with her. Many others did not. Some people believed her ideas would hurt the family. Friedan's book was a call to action. She lectured and wrote many articles. She became famous.

In 1966, Friedan and other **feminist** leaders formed the National Organization for Women (NOW). Friedan became its first president. NOW's goal was to fight sex discrimination. The Civil Rights Act of 1964 had banned sex discrimination. That meant that women and men were to be treated equally in the workplace. However, the government was not enforcing the law. Newspapers listed job ads separately for men and women. Airlines often fired female flight attendants who got married. NOW worked to end these and other unfair practices.

Protesters march for women's rights.

Within 5 years, NOW grew from 28 members to more than 15,000. It became powerful. During national elections, NOW members' votes became important. Candidates took on their issues.

Meet | Gloria Steinem

In 1972, Gloria Steinem and a partner founded *Ms.*, a feminist magazine. In 1993, Steinem, a journalist and writer, was inducted into the National Women's Hall of Fame in Seneca Falls, N.Y. She has supported the United Farm Workers and worked for civil rights.

The Triumph of Title IX

Title IX made school sports equally available to female and male students.

Women won an important battle with the passage of Title IX in 1972. Title IX was a federal law that said schools and colleges could not discriminate in any school activities, including sports and educational programs. If a school did discriminate, it would no longer receive money from the federal government.

Many schools had offered sports only for boys and men. With Title IX in place, they now had to offer the same programs for girls and women.

Before Title IX, only 1 in 27 high school girls played sports. Today, one in three girls plays sports. More girls have become good athletes. As a result, colleges give more scholarships to female athletes than they once did. Title IX has helped many young women get a college education.

Voices from America

"If you grew up female in America, you heard this: Sports are unfeminine."

—MARIAH BURTON NELSON, author and former professional basketball player

The Equal Rights Amendment

After a struggle that began in 1848, American women won the right to vote in 1920. This right was granted with the passage of the Nineteenth Amendment to the Constitution. Soon after, many women began to fight for another amendment to the Constitution. Alice Paul wrote the Equal Rights Amendment (ERA) in 1923. It called for men and women to have equal rights. The amendment was first introduced in Congress that year. It was not approved.

ERA supporters at the Democratic National Convention in 1980

In 1967, Betty Friedan led NOW in a fight for the ERA. In 1971, Congress began to reconsider the amendment. The House and then the Senate approved it in 1972. Next, 38 states had to ratify, or approve, the ERA before it became law. The states needed to ratify the bill before time ran out in 1982. Only 35 states approved the ERA before the deadline. It did not pass.

Soon, however, states across the country passed laws banning job and educational discrimination against women. Today, such discrimination is not legal anywhere in the United States.

Meet | Alice Paul

In 1913, Alice Paul organized thousands of women to march in Washington, D.C., in support of the Nineteenth Amendment. Paul earned three law degrees during the 1920s. She wanted to know more about the law so she could campaign effectively for equal rights. Paul kept working for women's rights until she died in 1977.

Women's Victories and the Continuing Struggle

The Civil Rights Act of 1964 made sex discrimination in the workplace illegal. However, many employers did not want to hire women for certain types of jobs. Some employers continued to discriminate against their female employees. Women pressured the government to enforce the law. Soon, women had more job opportunities. Many women started their own businesses.

Today, many women are not paid as well as men who do the same jobs. Often, women are not promoted to top positions in business and industry. Women are not a minority group. They make up more than half the population of the United States. Yet, they do not hold half the leadership positions in this country.

Women have proven that they have a powerful political voice. They pushed to end sex discrimination. Thanks to them, it is no longer strange for girls to play sports. It is no longer unusual for women to become doctors and lawyers. Women today can enter the military or sit as judges on the highest courts in the land. Women still have much to do, but there are many of them, and they will be heard.

By 1993, 48 women were serving in Congress. Since then, women have served in important leadership roles in Congress.

Legacy

From 1955 through 1975, African Americans, Latinos, Native Americans, and women worked for equal rights. Some gave their lives to the cause.

The fight is not over, but much progress has been made. Today, more minorities and women receive a quality education and a college degree than was possible 50 years ago. More minorities and women hold political offices and have better jobs and better housing. More people take pride in their own culture and believe that they can change things.

Since 1975, other minorities, newly arrived in the United States, have faced discrimination. So, people are still working to make sure that all Americans have equal rights, just as the Constitution says they do.

Protesters march on Washington in 1963.

Glossary

activist a person in favor of taking strong, direct action to get political or social change

assassinate to murder a public figure usually for political reasons

bilingual using two languages

boycott the act of refusing to buy or use something as a way of making a protest

civil rights the individual rights that all members of a society have to freedom and equal treatment under the law

demonstration a public meeting or march to protest or make demands

desegregate to end the practice of separating people of different races in public places

discrimination unfair treatment of people because of differences, especially in race, gender, or religion

feminist someone who believes strongly that women ought to have the same opportunities and rights that men have

lobbyist a person who works to persuade politicians to act or vote in a certain way

marshal a federal officer who carries out court orders

migrant a person who travels from one place to another in search of work

minority a group of people of a particular race, ethnic group, or religion living among a larger group of a different race, ethnic group, or religion

ratify to agree to or approve officially

reservation an area of land set aside by the government for a special purpose

segregation the act or practice of keeping people or groups apart

sit-in an organized demonstration in which people seat themselves and refuse to move in protest of racial discrimination

unconstitutional not in agreement with the Constitution

Index